Drawing on years of real-world experience and proven success strategies, this book will revolutionize the way you approach your SaaS business. Whether you're a startup founder or an established entrepreneur, SaaS Success Secrets is the key to unlocking your business's potential and achieving sustainable growth.

SAAS SUCCESS SECRETS:

Chapter I

Identify Your Niche: Finding a Profitable Idea for a SAAS Business

When starting a Software as a Service (SAAS) business, one of the most crucial steps is identifying your niche. A niche is a specific segment of the market that you will cater to with your product or service. By targeting a niche, you can differentiate yourself from competitors and position your SAAS business for success. In this article, we will explore the importance of identifying your niche and provide a clear decisive way to ensure you find a profitable idea.

Why Identifying Your Niche is Important

Identifying your niche is important for several reasons. Firstly, it helps you understand who your target audience is and what their specific pain points are. By specializing in a particular market segment, you can tailor your product to address the unique needs and challenges of your customers. This targeted approach increases the chances of attracting and retaining customers who resonate with your offering.

Secondly, identifying your niche enables you to differentiate yourself from competitors. In the crowded SAAS market, standing out is essential for success. By focusing on a specific niche, you can highlight the unique value proposition of your product and position yourself as an expert in solving the problems faced by customers within that niche.

Finally, targeting a niche allows you to optimize your marketing efforts. Instead of casting a wide net and trying to reach everyone, you can concentrate your resources on a specific group of customers who are more likely to be interested in and benefit from your product. This targeted marketing approach can lead to higher conversion rates and a more efficient use of your marketing budget.

How to Find a Profitable Idea

Now that we understand the importance of identifying a niche for your SAAS business, let's explore a clear decisive way to find a profitable idea.

Market Research: Start by conducting comprehensive market research to identify existing gaps and opportunities within the SAAS industry. Look for industries or sectors that are experiencing growth or undergoing digital transformation, as they are more likely to have a demand for innovative SAAS solutions. Analyze market trends, competitor offerings, and customer feedback to gain insights into what works and what doesn't.

Identify Pain Points: Talk to potential customers, industry experts, and professionals within the niche you are considering. Understand their pain points, challenges, and unmet needs. By empathizing with your target audience, you can identify the most pressing problems they face and uncover opportunities for your SAAS business to provide solutions.

Evaluate Competition: Study your competitors within the niche. Analyze their strengths, weaknesses, and gaps in their offerings. Look for areas where you can differentiate yourself or provide a better solution. Identifying underserved or unsatisfied customer segments will give you a competitive advantage and increase your chances of success.

Define Your Unique Value Proposition: Based on your market research and understanding of customer pain points, define your unique value proposition. This is the clear and compelling reason why customers should choose your product over competitors. Your value proposition should highlight the benefits and advantages your SAAS solution offers and articulate how it solves the specific challenges of your target audience.

Validate Your Idea: Once you have identified a potential niche and developed a concept for your SAAS product, it is essential to validate your idea before investing significant time and resources. Create a prototype or minimum viable product (MVP) to test the market and gather feedback from your target audience. Iterate and refine your product based on this feedback until you have a solution that resonates with your customers.

Analyze Profitability: Assess the profitability of your potential niche by analyzing the market size, demand, and revenue potential. Consider factors such as the willingness to pay, customer acquisition costs, and lifetime value of customers within the niche. Conduct a thorough financial analysis to ensure that your SAAS business idea has the potential to be profitable in the long run.

By following these steps, you can increase your chances of finding a profitable niche for your SAAS business.

Identifying your niche is a critical step in starting a SAAS business. It helps you understand your target audience, differentiate yourself from competitors, and optimize your marketing efforts. By conducting market research, identifying pain points, evaluating competition, defining your unique value proposition, validating your idea, and analyzing profitability, you can find a profitable niche for your SAAS business. Remember to stay customer-centric and adapt your product to meet the specific needs of your target audience.

Chapter II

Choose Your SAAS Platform: Exploring Pros and Cons of Different Options

When starting a Software as a Service (SAAS) business, choosing the right SAAS platform is a crucial decision. The platform you select will determine the ease of development, scalability, and overall success of your SAAS product. In this article, we will explore the pros and cons of several popular SAAS platforms to help you make an informed choice.

1. Bubble.io
Pros:
Visual No-Code Development: Bubble.io offers a visual, drag-and-drop interface that allows you to build complex web applications without writing code. This makes it user-friendly for entrepreneurs without extensive coding knowledge.
Rapid Development: Bubble.io enables rapid prototyping and development, reducing time to market. You can create proof-of-concepts and MVPs quickly, allowing for iterative improvements.
Built-in Database and Backend: Bubble.io provides a built-in database and backend infrastructure, eliminating the need for additional services. This simplifies the development process and reduces costs.

Cons:
Learning Curve: While Bubble.io is no-code, it still has a learning curve. Users must invest time to understand its logic and features, especially for more complex applications.

Limited Customization: Although Bubble.io offers various customization options, there may be limitations in terms of design flexibility compared to fully custom-coded solutions.
Reliance on Platform: As a SAAS platform itself, your business will rely on Bubble.io's availability and continued support. Any issues or changes to the platform could impact your product.

2. Webflow
Pros:
Powerful Web Design: Webflow is known for its advanced web design capabilities, offering a high level of customization and control over the frontend experience.
Responsive Design: Webflow enables you to create websites that automatically adjust to different screen sizes, providing a seamless user experience across devices.
Hosting Included: Webflow provides hosting services, making it convenient to publish and manage your SAAS product without the need for separate hosting arrangements.

Cons:
Learning Curve and Complexity: Webflow has a steeper learning curve, especially for beginners. Its advanced features and flexibility require time and effort to fully understand and utilize.
Less Backend Functionality: While Webflow excels in frontend design, it may have limitations when it comes to complex backend functionalities. Additional backend services or custom coding may be required.
Pricing: Webflow's pricing structure can be perceived as expensive for some startups, especially if you need to access certain features or want to scale your product rapidly.

3. Adalo

Pros:

Mobile App Development: Adalo specializes in mobile app development, allowing you to create cross-platform apps without coding. It has ready-made templates and components specifically tailored for mobile applications.

Native Look and Feel: Adalo apps have a native look and feel, providing a seamless experience for users. This can enhance user engagement and create a professional impression.

Integration Capabilities: Adalo offers integration with various third-party services, allowing you to connect your application with popular tools and platforms.

Cons:

Limited Web App Support: While Adalo focuses on mobile app development, it may have limitations if you also require a web app alongside your mobile presence.

Customization Restrictions: Adalo offers customization options, but they may be more limited compared to fully custom-coded solutions. This can restrict certain design or functionality choices.

Learning Curve for Advanced Features: While Adalo is no-code, more advanced features or complex functionality may require additional learning and understanding of the platform.

4. Glide

Pros:

Google Sheets Integration: Glide's standout feature is its integration with Google Sheets. This allows you to use spreadsheets as your backend database, which can be convenient for certain applications.

Easy Data Management: Glide simplifies data management by automatically handling data

syncing between your app and Google Sheets.
This makes it easy to update and maintain app
content.
Quick Prototyping: Glide enables rapid
prototyping, allowing you to quickly create
functional app prototypes to gather user
feedback and validate your ideas.

Cons:
Design Limitations: Glide's design options may
be more limited compared to other platforms,
impacting the visual aesthetics and
customization of your app.
Limited Backend Functionality: While Glide is
suitable for building simple to moderately
complex apps, it may have limitations when it
comes to advanced backend functionalities or
complex business logic.
Reliance on Google Sheets: As with any platform
relying on a third-party service, any changes or
issues with Google Sheets could affect your
app's functionality. It's important to consider the
stability and reliability of the underlying service.

Choosing the right SAAS platform is vital for your
business's success. Each platform, whether
Bubble.io, Webflow, Adalo, or Glide, comes with
its own set of pros and cons. Consider factors
such as your technical expertise, design
requirements, backend functionality needs,
scalability, and budget when making your
decision. By understanding the strengths and
limitations of each platform, you can make an
informed choice that aligns with your SAAS
business goals and objectives.

Chapter III

Developing a Prototype/Minimum Viable Product (MVP): A Step-by-Step Guide

Developing a prototype or minimum viable product (MVP) is a crucial step in testing the viability of your idea and ensuring that you have a working concept for market and sale. This process involves creating an early, simplified version of your product that helps you identify and address potential flaws or issues before investing heavily in development.

To help you develop an effective prototype/MVP, here is a step-by-step guide on how to test the viability of your idea and create a working prototype for your SAAS business.

1. Define Your Idea and Target Audience

The first step in developing a prototype/MVP is to define your idea and target audience. Start by identifying a clear problem that your SAAS business aims to solve, and research your target audience to understand their needs and preferences. Use this information to create a detailed plan for your prototype/MVP that outlines the features and functionality you will need to develop.

2. Choose a Development Process

There are several approaches to developing a prototype/MVP, including no-code tools, low-code tools, and custom development. Each approach has its own benefits and limitations, so it's important to choose an option that aligns with your goals, timeline, and budget.

No-code tools: No-code tools are ideal for entrepreneurs that don't have extensive coding knowledge. These platforms allow you to create a prototype/MVP using drag-and-drop or visual interfaces.

Low-code tools: Low-code tools are a step up from no-code platforms, offering more customization and flexibility without requiring extensive coding knowledge. These platforms usually offer pre-built libraries and templates to help speed up development.

Custom development: Custom development involves hiring a development team to build your prototype/MVP from scratch. While this approach can be more expensive, it offers the most flexibility and customization options.

3. Build Your Prototype/MVP

Once you have chosen a development process, it's time to build your prototype/MVP. The following steps outline a general process that can be adapted to suit your specific situation:

Design Your User Interface (UI): Develop a wireframe or prototype of your application's UI, keeping it simple and easy-to-use. This will give you a tangible representation of your product and allow you to test usability.

Develop Core Features: Develop core features that address the primary problem your product aims to solve. This will help you identify and address essential functionality early on, rather than wasting time and resources on less important features.

Implement Testing: Create a testing plan that outlines the key areas of functionality to test, and specify the testing criteria that will be used. Ideally, you should test your prototype/MVP with

a small sample group of users to gather feedback and make improvements iteratively. Refine and Improve: Based on your testing and feedback, refine and improve your prototype/MVP. Iterate on features, adjust design elements, and make critical changes to ensure that your product meets the needs of your target audience.
4. Launch Your Prototype/MVP

After completing the development and testing phase, it's time to launch your prototype/MVP. While launching your SAAS product is an exciting milestone, it's important to remain focused on gathering and integrating feedback to improve your product.

Gather Feedback: Launch your prototype/MVP to a small group of users, and gather feedback as you continue to develop and iterate. Use this feedback to identify areas for improvement and make modifications as needed.
Monitor Metrics: Keep an eye on key metrics such as engagement, conversion rates, and user satisfaction. This will help you identify where your product is succeeding and areas of potential weakness to address.
Scale Gradually: Don't try to scale too quickly. Gradually expand your user base and functionality to ensure that your product remains stable and reliable.

Chapter IIV

Define your business model

Defining your business model is a crucial step in starting a successful business. A business model defines how your company generates revenue, creates value for customers, and operates in the marketplace. In this 800-word article, we will cover how to define your business model, including market research, pricing your product, and setting up revenue streams.

Market Research

Market research is the process of gathering data on your target market and competitors. The purpose of market research is to gain insight into customer behavior, market trends, and competition in your industry. Market research is essential to defining your business model because it helps you understand your target market and identify opportunities for growth.

The first step in market research is identifying your target market. Start by developing a buyer persona that represents your ideal customer. This persona should include demographic information such as age, gender, location, and income, as well as psychographic information such as interests, lifestyle, and values. Understanding your target market helps you tailor your product or service to meet their needs, wants, and preferences.

The second step in market research is analyzing your competition. Identifying and analyzing your competitors helps you understand their strengths and weaknesses, how they are positioning themselves in the market, and how you can differentiate yourself from them. Look at their marketing strategies, product offerings, pricing, and business model to gain insights into how they operate and what you can learn from them.

The third step in market research is conducting surveys, focus groups, or interviews with potential customers. This feedback helps you refine your product or service, messaging, and marketing strategies to better align with your target market's needs and preferences.

Pricing Strategies

Once you have completed your market research, the next step is to develop a pricing strategy for your product or service. Pricing is a critical component of your business model because it directly impacts your revenue streams and profitability.

The first step in developing a pricing strategy is to identify your costs. This includes the direct costs of producing your product or service, as well as indirect costs such as salaries, marketing expenses, and overhead. Understanding your costs helps you determine the minimum price you need to charge to break even.

The second step in pricing is to analyze your market and competition. Look at the prices your competitors are charging for similar products or services and how customers are responding to those prices. This information helps you determine where to position your product or service in the market and whether to charge a premium or discount price.

The third step in pricing is to consider pricing strategies such as cost-plus, value-based, or dynamic pricing. Cost-plus pricing involves adding a markup to your costs to determine the price. Value-based pricing considers how much value your product or service provides to the customer and charges accordingly. Dynamic pricing adjusts the price based on market demand, such as surge pricing for ride-sharing services during peak hours.

Revenue Streams

Revenue streams are the sources of income generated by your business. Defining your revenue streams is an essential component of your business model because it helps you identify how your business generates revenue and how to optimize profitability.

The first step in defining your revenue streams is to identify the different types of revenues you can generate. This includes sales revenue from selling your product or service, subscription revenue from recurring billing, advertising revenue from sponsorships or partnerships, and referral or affiliate revenue from promoting other companies' products or services.

The second step in defining your revenue streams is to analyze your market and competition. Understand how your competitors generate revenue and how customers are shopping for products or services in your industry. This information helps you identify which revenue streams are the most attractive and how to optimize your revenue streams for profitability.

The third step in defining your revenue streams is to prioritize and test revenue streams. Not all revenue streams are equally effective, and some may not work for your business model or target market. Test different revenue streams to see which ones generate the most revenue and optimize accordingly.

Conclusion

In conclusion, defining your business model is a critical step in starting a successful business. Market research helps you understand your target market and competitors, pricing defines how you generate revenue and profitability, and revenue streams identify different sources of income. By combining these three elements, you can develop a sustainable and profitable business model that creates value for customers and grows your business. Remember to regularly reassess and update your business model to adapt to changes in your industry and market conditions.

Chapter V

Developing Your Branding

Developing a strong brand is a crucial aspect of building a successful business. Your brand represents your values, personality, and mission, and it can differentiate you from your competitors. Developing a successful brand requires a multifaceted approach that encompasses everything from market research to visual design elements. In this article, we will provide a comprehensive guide on how to develop your branding and cultivate a strong and recognizable brand identity.

1. Define Your Brand

The first step in developing your branding is to define your brand. Your brand should align with your business goals, values, and mission. Start by defining your brand's personality and tone - is it playful, professional, or technical?

Next, consider what sets your brand apart from your competitors. What makes your product or service unique, and how can you communicate that value to your customers? Be sure to identify your brand's target audience and consider their values and preferences when developing your brand identity.

2. Research Your Market and Competitors

Market research is essential to understanding your customers and your competitors. Conduct research on your target audience and their needs and preferences. Consider conducting surveys or focus groups to gather quantitative and qualitative data.

Additionally, research your competitors to understand their positioning, value propositions, and branding. Use this information to identify gaps in the market and differentiate your brand from others in your industry.

3. Develop Your Visual Identity

Your visual identity includes everything from your logo and color scheme to your website design and promotional materials. It's essential to develop a visual identity that aligns with your brand personality and resonates with your target audience.

Start by creating a logo that is distinctive, memorable, and visually appealing. Use color psychology to select a color scheme that communicates the right emotions and tone for your brand. Consider hiring a graphic designer to create high-quality visuals for your website, social media channels, and marketing materials.

4. Create Your Brand Message

Your brand message is the central message you use to communicate with your audience. It should be concise, clear, and easy to understand. Use your brand message to articulate your value proposition and mission statement.

When creating your brand message, consider your audience's needs and preferences. Your message should resonate with them and address their pain points or needs.

5. Build Your Brand Across Channels

Building your brand across channels is essential to creating a consistent and recognizable brand identity. Your branding should extend across all customer touchpoints, including your website, social media channels, promotional materials, and customer support.

Use consistent visual elements and messaging to ensure that your brand is recognizable across all channels. Additionally, choose channels that align with your target audience's preferences and habits. For example, if your audience is predominantly using Instagram, focus your branding efforts on that platform.

6. Maintain Your Brand Identity

Maintaining your brand identity requires ongoing effort and consistency over time. Be sure to regularly review and update your branding elements to ensure they align with your evolving business goals and audience's needs.

Additionally, monitoring customer feedback and engagement can help you identify areas of your branding that may need improvement. Use this feedback to continually refine and improve your branding strategy.

Developing a strong brand is critical to building a successful business. By defining your brand, researching your market and competitors, developing a visual identity, creating your brand message, building your brand across channels, and maintaining your brand identity consistently over time, you can create a strong and recognizable brand that resonates with your target audience. Remember to use market research and customer feedback to inform your branding decisions, and don't be afraid to evolve and adapt your branding strategy over time to meet changing market and customer needs.

Chapter VI

Writing a Business Plan and Marketing Strategy

Developing a business plan and marketing strategy is crucial to the success of any business. A well-crafted plan outlines your goals, target audience, competition, and marketing approach. In this guide, we will provide a step-by-step process on how to research and develop a strong business plan and marketing strategy that will set your business on the path to success.

1. Research Your Market

Before writing a business plan and marketing strategy, it's important to thoroughly research your market. Understand your target audience, their needs, preferences, and behaviors. Conduct market research to gather data on industry trends, market size, and customer demographics.

Furthermore, research your competitors. Identify their strengths, weaknesses, and market positioning. This will help you differentiate your business and develop a competitive advantage.

2. Define Your Business Goals

Start by defining clear and specific business goals. What do you want to achieve in the short-term and long-term? Ensure that your goals are measurable and realistic. This will provide a foundation for your marketing strategy and help you stay focused on your objectives.

3. Identify Your Target Audience

Clearly define your target audience. Develop buyer personas that represent your ideal customers, including demographics, behaviors, motivations, and pain points. Understanding your target audience will help tailor your marketing efforts and ensure your message resonates with the right people.

4. Develop Your Unique Value Proposition

A unique value proposition (UVP) is a statement that articulates the unique benefits customers will receive from choosing your product or service over alternatives. Identify what sets you apart from your competitors and craft a compelling UVP that captures the essence of your business.

5. Conduct a SWOT Analysis

Performing a SWOT (Strengths, Weaknesses, Opportunities, Threats) analysis helps assess internal and external factors that may impact your business. Identify your strengths, weaknesses, opportunities for growth, and potential threats from competitors or market changes. This analysis will inform your marketing strategy and help you capitalize on your strengths while mitigating weaknesses and threats.

6. Develop Your Marketing Objectives and Strategies

Based on your research and analysis, define your marketing objectives. These objectives should be specific, measurable, achievable, relevant, and time-bound (SMART). For example, your objective may be to increase online sales by 20% within the next six months.

Next, outline the strategies you will employ to achieve your marketing objectives. These strategies could include digital marketing, content marketing, social media marketing, email marketing, influencer partnerships, or traditional advertising. Tailor your strategies to reach your target audience effectively.

7. Determine Your Marketing Budget

Allocating a budget for marketing activities is essential. Determine how much you are willing to invest in marketing and allocate funds to different channels and strategies. Consider the potential return on investment (ROI) for each marketing tactic and prioritize accordingly.

8. Create a Marketing Plan

Now that you have defined your marketing objectives, strategies, and budget, it's time to develop a comprehensive marketing plan. This plan should include:

Target audience: Clearly define your target audience, emphasizing their demographics, behaviors, and preferences.
Branding: Outline your brand identity, including your logo, color scheme, tone of voice, and key messages.
Marketing channels: Identify the marketing channels you will utilize, such as social media platforms, websites, email marketing, and advertising channels.

Content strategy: Develop a content strategy that provides value to your audience and aligns with your brand messaging.
Promotion and advertising: Specify the promotional tactics and advertising methods you will employ to reach your target audience effectively.
Budget: Clearly outline your marketing budget, including how much you will allocate to each marketing channel and activity.
Timeline: Create a timeline for your marketing activities and identify key milestones and deadlines.
Key performance indicators (KPIs): Determine the metrics you will measure to assess the success of your marketing efforts.

9. Write Your Business Plan

Now that you have developed your marketing strategy, it's time to write your business plan. A comprehensive business plan typically includes the following sections:

Executive summary: Provides an overview of your business, including its mission, vision, and goals.
Company description: Offers a detailed description of your business, its history, legal structure, and products or services.
Market analysis: Presents your market research findings, including industry trends, target audience analysis, and competitor analysis.
Organization and management: Provides information about the structure of your organization, key team members, and their roles.
Products or services: Describes your offerings, features, benefits, and unique selling points.

Marketing and sales: Outlines your marketing strategy, including target audience, distribution channels, pricing, branding, and promotional activities.

Financial projections: Presents financial forecasts, including revenue projections, expenses, and cash flow analysis.

Funding request (if applicable): Specifies the funding you require to start or grow your business and how it will be utilized.

Conclusion: Summarizes your business plan and reiterates your mission, goals, and strategies.

10. Continuously Evaluate and Adjust

Remember that your business plan and marketing strategy are not set in stone. Continuously evaluate the performance of your marketing activities and make adjustments as needed. Monitor key performance indicators and be open to adapting your tactics based on customer feedback and market changes.

Developing a business plan and marketing strategy is an essential step in ensuring the success of your business. By conducting market research, defining business goals, identifying your target audience, crafting a unique value proposition, and developing a comprehensive marketing plan, you will set yourself up for growth and profitability. Regularly assess and adjust your strategies based on feedback and market conditions to stay ahead of the competition and meet your business objectives.

Chapter VII

Choosing Metrics to Track: Key Performance Indicators (KPIs) for Business Success

Tracking the performance of your business is crucial for making informed decisions and driving growth. By choosing the right key performance indicators (KPIs), you can measure and monitor the effectiveness of your strategies and tactics. In this chapter, we will explore popular metrics such as monthly recurring revenue (MRR), customer acquisition cost (CAC), customer lifetime value (LTV), and churn rate to help you track your business's performance effectively.

Monthly Recurring Revenue (MRR)

Monthly recurring revenue (MRR) is a key metric for subscription-based businesses. It represents the predictable revenue stream from your subscriptions on a monthly basis. MRR allows you to understand the stability and growth potential of your business.

To calculate MRR, sum up the recurring revenue generated from all your active subscriptions. This includes monthly or annual subscription fees and any additional charges. By tracking MRR, you can identify trends and patterns in your revenue growth or decline, enabling you to make data-driven decisions to drive your business forward.

Monitoring MRR provides valuable insights into the effectiveness of your pricing, product offerings, and customer retention strategies. It helps you identify opportunities to upsell, cross-sell, or optimize your subscription plans to increase revenue and strengthen customer loyalty.

Customer Acquisition Cost (CAC)

Customer acquisition cost (CAC) is a metric that measures how much it costs to acquire a new customer. CAC takes into account all the costs associated with acquiring customers, including marketing expenses, sales commissions, advertising campaigns, and other related costs.

To calculate CAC, divide the total costs incurred in acquiring new customers during a given period by the number of customers acquired in that period. This provides you with a benchmark for evaluating the efficiency of your marketing and sales efforts.

Monitoring CAC helps you assess the effectiveness of your customer acquisition strategies and optimize your marketing spend. By comparing CAC to customer lifetime value (LTV), you can determine whether your marketing investments are generating a positive return on investment (ROI) or if adjustments are needed.

Customer Lifetime Value (LTV)

Customer lifetime value (LTV) is a metric that predicts the total revenue a customer is expected to generate throughout their relationship with your business. LTV helps you estimate the long-term value of acquiring and retaining a customer, allowing you to make informed decisions regarding customer acquisition and retention strategies.

Calculating LTV requires an estimation of the average revenue generated by each customer over their lifetime and multiplying it by the average customer lifespan. Additional factors to consider include customer retention rates, upsell and cross-sell opportunities, and customer churn rates.

LTV assists in prioritizing your resources and efforts towards acquiring high-value customers and retaining them over the long term. By increasing customer loyalty, delivering exceptional customer experiences, and identifying opportunities for upselling or cross-selling, you can maximize LTV and sustain profitability.

Churn Rate

Churn rate measures the rate at which customers stop using your product or service over a specific period. It is a critical metric for subscription-based businesses or those relying on recurring revenue streams.

Churn rate is calculated by dividing the number of customers who cancel or unsubscribe by the total number of customers at the beginning of the period. This percentage reflects customer attrition within that period.

Monitoring churn rate is essential for identifying and addressing potential issues that may be impacting customer retention. Retaining existing customers is often more cost-effective than acquiring new ones, making churn rate a significant indicator of business sustainability and growth.

High churn rates may suggest an issue with your product, service, or customer experience. By analyzing customer feedback, identifying pain points, and implementing strategies to improve customer satisfaction and retention, you can reduce churn and increase long-term revenue stability.

Choosing the Right Metrics and Tracking

When choosing the metrics to track for your business, consider the specific goals and objectives of your company. Select the KPIs that align with your business model, target audience, and long-term strategy.

To track your metrics effectively, consider using data analytics tools or customer relationship management systems (CRMs). These technologies can help automate data collection, visualization, and reporting, saving you time and providing real-time insights into your business's performance.

Regularly review and reassess your chosen metrics to ensure they remain relevant and aligned with your business goals. Tracking these metrics consistently over time will allow you to identify trends, make data-driven decisions, and optimize your strategies accordingly.

Choosing the right metrics and effectively tracking them is vital for evaluating the performance of your business. Metrics such as monthly recurring revenue (MRR), customer acquisition cost (CAC), customer lifetime value (LTV), and churn rate provide valuable insights into the effectiveness of your strategies and tactics.

By regularly monitoring these KPIs, you can make informed decisions, optimize your marketing and sales efforts, and improve customer retention. Remember, selecting the right metrics that align with your business goals is essential, and leveraging data analytics tools can simplify the process of tracking and analyzing these metrics.

Ensure that you review and analyze your metrics consistently, allowing you to adapt and make necessary adjustments to drive your business's growth and success. With the right KPIs in place, you can stay on top of your business's performance and make data-driven decisions that will contribute to its sustainable growth.

Chapter VIII

Test Your Product and Gather Feedback

Testing your product thoroughly is an essential step to ensure its functionality, robustness, and user satisfaction. In this chapter, we will explore the significance of product testing and the benefits of soliciting feedback from beta testers.

Importance of Product Testing
Testing your product allows you to identify and address any issues or shortcomings before releasing it to the market. It ensures that your product works as intended, meets user expectations, and provides an optimal user experience. Here are a few key reasons why product testing is crucial:

Identify and Fix Bugs: Testing helps you discover and rectify any bugs or technical glitches in your product. By resolving these issues in the testing phase, you can minimize the chances of them occurring post-launch.

Ensure Feature Completeness: Thorough testing ensures that all the necessary features and functionalities are included in your product. It allows you to validate that every aspect of your product is working as intended and meets the needs of your target audience.

Optimize Performance: By testing your product's performance under various conditions, you can identify and optimize areas that may be causing delays, crashes, or other performance issues. This helps you deliver a seamless and efficient user experience.

Enhance User Satisfaction: By testing your product with real users, you can gather feedback and make improvements that enhance user satisfaction. Identifying and addressing user pain points or frustrations improves the overall quality and usability of your product.

Testing Methodologies
To test your product effectively, you can employ various testing methodologies. Here are a few commonly used approaches:

Unit Testing: Unit testing involves testing individual components or modules of your product to ensure they function correctly. By isolating each component, you can identify and fix any issues before integrating them into the larger system.

Integration Testing: Integration testing focuses on testing how different components interact and function together. It ensures that the integration of various parts of your product doesn't introduce any new issues or conflicts.

User Acceptance Testing: User acceptance testing involves testing your product with real users to gauge their satisfaction and gather feedback. This type of testing helps validate if your product meets user expectations and if any adjustments are needed.

Performance Testing: Performance testing assesses your product's responsiveness, reliability, and stability under various workloads or stress conditions. It helps you optimize your product's performance and ensures it can handle the expected demand.

Security Testing: Security testing helps identify vulnerabilities and potential security threats in your product. This type of testing ensures that your product protects user data and maintains the necessary security standards.

Leveraging Beta Testers
Soliciting feedback from beta testers is an excellent way to gather valuable insights and make informed decisions about your product. Beta testers are users who try out your product before its official launch and provide feedback on their experience.

Here are some benefits of involving beta testers in your product testing:

Real-World Feedback: Beta testers can provide you with real-world feedback on how users interact with your product. They can identify potential usability issues, provide insights into their preferences, and suggest improvements.

Identify Undetected Issues: Beta testers often uncover issues or bugs that were not identified during internal testing. Their unique perspectives and diverse usage patterns can reveal overlooked problems that you can fix before the product launch.

User Persona Validation: Beta testers represent your target audience, allowing you to validate if your product resonates with them. Their feedback helps you ensure that your product meets their needs and aligns with their expectations.

Word-of-Mouth Marketing: Engaging beta testers can turn them into advocates for your product. If they have a positive experience during testing, they are more likely to share their excitement and anticipation with others, generating buzz for your upcoming launch.

Enhanced User Adoption: By incorporating beta testers' feedback into your product improvements, you increase the chances of users adopting and embracing your product. Addressing their concerns and incorporating their suggestions shows your commitment to providing a top-notch user experience.

Best Practices for Gathering Feedback
To make the most out of your beta testing phase, follow these best practices for gathering feedback:

Define Clear Objectives: Outline the specific objectives you want to achieve through the beta testing phase. Clearly communicate these objectives to your beta testers so they can provide feedback that aligns with your goals.

Provide Clear Instructions: Clearly explain the purpose of the beta testing and inform your testers about the expected behavior and tasks to complete. This will ensure consistency in the testing process and help you gather relevant feedback.

Use Feedback Channels: Establish channels for beta testers to provide feedback, such as a dedicated feedback form, email, or discussion forum. Make it easy for them to share their thoughts and encourage open communication.

Encourage Detailed Feedback: Encourage beta testers to provide specific and constructive feedback. Ask them to share their experience, identify areas for improvement, and suggest possible solutions.

Regularly Communicate Updates: Keep your beta testers informed about any updates or improvements you make based on their feedback. This reinforces their role in the process and demonstrates your commitment to continuous improvement.

Thoroughly testing your product and gathering feedback from beta testers are crucial steps in ensuring its success. Product testing allows you to identify and resolve issues, optimize performance, and enhance user satisfaction. Beta testers provide valuable feedback from the perspective of real users, helping you make informed decisions and improvements.

By implementing effective testing methodologies and leveraging beta testers, you can increase the quality and usability of your product. This, in turn, improves user adoption, drives positive word-of-mouth, and contributes to the success of your product in the market. So, don't underestimate the power of product testing and the valuable insights that beta testers can provide.

Chapter IX

Launch and Promote Your Product

Once you have thoroughly tested your product and gathered feedback from beta testers, it's time to launch and promote your product. The success of your launch can significantly impact your product's adoption and revenue generation. In this chapter, we will explore the strategies to effectively launch your product and promote it through various channels.

Launching Your Product
Launching your product involves making it available to the public and creating a buzz around its release. Here are some essential steps to ensure a successful launch:

Set Launch Goals: Define clear goals for your launch, such as acquiring a certain number of customers, generating a specific amount of revenue, or achieving a high number of product downloads. Having well-defined goals provides direction and helps measure the success of your launch.

Create Launch Materials: Develop compelling launch materials, such as press releases, demo videos, screenshots, and product documentation. These materials should effectively communicate the value proposition of your product and generate excitement among potential customers.

Build Anticipation: Before the official launch, create a sense of anticipation by teasing your product through social media posts, blog articles, and email newsletters. Generate curiosity by sharing sneak peeks, product features, or testimonials from beta testers.

Plan Launch Events: Consider organizing virtual or in-person launch events to amplify your product's visibility. These events can include webinars, product demos, or live Q&A sessions. Engage with your audience during these events, answer their questions, and showcase the unique benefits of your product.

Prepare Launch Assets: Make sure your website and other online platforms are updated with relevant launch assets, such as landing pages, product descriptions, pricing information, and call-to-action buttons. Ensure that these assets are user-friendly and provide a seamless experience for potential customers.

Promoting Your Product
Once your product is launched, it's important to promote it effectively to reach your target audience and attract customers. Here are some strategies to consider:

Social Media Marketing: Leverage popular social media platforms, such as Facebook, Twitter, LinkedIn, and Instagram, to promote your product. Create engaging posts, share updates, and interact with your audience. Utilize paid advertising options on these platforms to expand your reach even further.

Email Marketing: Build an email list of interested prospects and existing customers who may be interested in your product. Send out targeted email campaigns to promote your product, highlighting its unique features, benefits, and any current promotions or discounts.

Content Marketing: Develop valuable and informative content, such as blog articles, whitepapers, case studies, or videos, that showcase your product and provide value to your target audience. Share this content on your website, social media profiles, and industry-related platforms to establish yourself as an authority in your field.

Influencer Marketing: Collaborate with influencers or industry experts with a substantial following to promote your product. They can create sponsored content, reviews, or tutorials that reach their audience and generate interest in your product. Ensure that the influencers align with your brand and target audience.

Paid Advertising: Utilize paid advertising options, such as Google Ads or display ads on relevant websites, to increase product visibility and reach a wider audience. Target your ads based on user demographics, interests, and search behavior to maximize their effectiveness.

Referral Programs: Implement a referral program that incentivizes existing customers to refer your product to others. Offer rewards, discounts, or exclusive access to new features as incentives. This can help generate organic word-of-mouth promotion and expand your customer base.

Monitoring and Analyzing Results
To gauge the effectiveness of your product launch and promotional efforts, it's important to monitor and analyze key metrics. This will help you understand what strategies are working well and where improvements can be made. Here are some metrics to consider:

Website and Landing Page Analytics: Monitor website traffic, bounce rate, conversion rate, and time on page to evaluate the effectiveness of your website and landing pages.

Social Media Engagement: Track engagement metrics such as likes, comments, shares, and click-through rates on your social media posts. Analyze which types of content resonate the most with your audience.

Email Campaign Performance: Measure the open rate, click-through rate, and conversion rate of your email campaigns. Experiment with different subject lines, call-to-action buttons, and content formats to optimize performance.

Conversion Funnel Analysis: Analyze the performance of your conversion funnel, from initial awareness to complete product purchase or sign-up. Identify any drop-off points and optimize your funnel to improve conversion rates.

Customer Feedback: Gather feedback from new customers about their experience with your product and the effectiveness of your promotional efforts. Implement surveys, user reviews, and customer interviews to gather valuable insights for future improvements.

Adapting and Iterating
Launching and promoting your product is an ongoing process, and it's important to adapt and iterate based on the insights you gather. Here are a few key points to consider:

Listen to Customer Feedback: Pay close attention to the feedback and suggestions provided by your customers. Use this feedback to make improvements, refine your messaging, and enhance your product's value proposition.

Monitor Competitors: Keep an eye on your competitors and how they promote their products. Leverage competitive analysis to identify any gaps in the market and differentiate your product from the competition.

Continuously Improve Marketing Efforts: Regularly assess the performance of your marketing strategies and adjust accordingly. Experiment with different techniques, explore new channels, and refine your messaging to optimize your promotional efforts.

Stay Connected with Your Audience: Engage with your audience through social media, email newsletters, and customer support channels. Regularly communicate updates, new features, and relevant industry information to maintain a strong relationship with your customers.

Launching and promoting your product is a dynamic and iterative process that requires a strategic approach and continuous refinement. By following an effective launch plan, leveraging various marketing channels, and monitoring key metrics, you can attract customers, increase monthly recurring revenue, and establish a strong foundation for the growth of your product. Remember to listen to your customers, adapt your strategies, and continuously improve to ensure long-term success in the market.

Chapter X

Continuously Evaluate and Improve Your Product

In today's rapidly changing business landscape, it is crucial for companies to continuously evaluate and improve their products to stay ahead of the competition. By consistently monitoring business metrics and gathering customer feedback, you can identify areas for improvement and optimize your product to meet the evolving needs and expectations of your customers. In this chapter, we will explore the importance of continuous evaluation and improvement and discuss strategies for effectively iterating on your product.

The Importance of Continuous Evaluation and Improvement
Continuously evaluating your business metrics and gathering customer feedback is essential for the long-term success of your product. Here are some reasons why continuous evaluation and improvement are crucial:

Identify Areas for Improvement: By regularly analyzing business metrics and customer feedback, you can identify areas of your product that may be underperforming or could be enhanced. This allows you to prioritize and address these areas, leading to a better user experience and higher customer satisfaction.

Stay Ahead of the Competition: The business landscape is constantly evolving, and competitors are continually innovating. By continuously evaluating and improving your product, you can stay ahead of the competition and remain relevant in the market. This ensures that your product continues to meet the changing needs and expectations of your customers.

Increase Customer Satisfaction: Customer satisfaction is crucial for the success of any product. By actively seeking and incorporating customer feedback into your product development process, you can address pain points, implement desired features, and provide a better overall experience for your customers. This, in turn, leads to increased customer satisfaction and loyalty.

Maximize Revenue and Growth: A well-improved product that meets the needs of your target market is more likely to attract new customers and retain existing ones. By continuously evaluating and improving your product, you can maximize revenue and drive sustained growth for your business.

Strategies for Continuous Evaluation and Improvement
To effectively evaluate and improve your product, you need to implement strategies that foster a culture of continuous improvement within your organization. Here are some strategies to consider:

Establish Key Performance Indicators (KPIs): Define key performance indicators that align with your business goals and product objectives. These KPIs should be measurable and provide insights into the performance of your product. Examples of KPIs could include customer acquisition cost, customer retention rate, monthly active users, or average revenue per user. Regularly monitor these KPIs to gauge the effectiveness of your product and identify areas for improvement.

Gather and Analyze Customer Feedback: Actively seek feedback from your customers through surveys, customer interviews, user testing, or online reviews. Analyze this feedback to identify common themes and pain points. Prioritize the feedback based on its impact on customer experience and potential business value. This feedback can be instrumental in guiding product improvements and ensuring customer satisfaction.

Implement Agile Development Practices: Adopt agile development practices that allow for continuous iteration and improvement. Break down your product roadmap into smaller, manageable increments that can be developed, tested, and released quickly. Implement feedback loops within your development process to incorporate customer feedback and adjust your product roadmap accordingly. This agile approach promotes flexibility, adaptability, and responsiveness to market needs.

Conduct A/B Testing: A/B testing involves comparing two or more variations of a feature, design, or user interface to determine which performs better. By conducting A/B tests, you can objectively evaluate and compare different options within your product. This allows you to make data-driven decisions and optimize your product based on user preferences and behavior.

Monitor User Analytics: Utilize user analytics tools to gather data on user behavior within your product. This data can provide valuable insights into how users interact with your product, which features are most used, and where users may be encountering difficulties. Regularly analyze user analytics to identify patterns, uncover usability issues, and iterate on your product to improve the overall user experience.

Encourage a Feedback Culture: Foster a feedback culture within your organization where all team members are encouraged to provide feedback and suggestions for improvement. This includes not only gathering feedback from customers but also valuing the insights and ideas of your employees. Regularly hold feedback sessions, conduct retrospective meetings, and establish open channels of communication to ensure that feedback is effectively shared and actioned upon.

Embrace Continuous Learning: Encourage your team members to continuously learn and stay updated on the latest industry trends and best practices. This can be done through attending conferences, participating in webinars, or providing training opportunities. By keeping your team members informed and knowledgeable, you can drive innovation, creativity, and continuous improvement within your organization.

Continuously Iterating and Improving Your Product
Once you have gathered feedback and identified areas for improvement, it's important to take action and iterate on your product. Here's a

step-by-step approach to effectively iterate and improve your product:

Prioritize Improvement Areas: Based on the feedback and data gathered, prioritize the areas that require improvement. Use a framework, such as the Impact vs. Effort matrix, to determine which improvements will have the most significant impact on customer experience and can be achieved with reasonable effort.

Define Actionable Steps: Break down the improvement areas into actionable steps or user stories. Clearly define the objectives, expectations, and success criteria for each step. This allows for better planning and implementation of the improvements.

Iterate in Small Increments: Adopt an iterative approach to implementing improvements. Rather than attempting to make all changes at once, break them down into smaller, manageable increments. This allows for faster implementation, quicker feedback loops, and the ability to adapt based on user responses.

Test and Measure Impact: Test the implemented improvements and gather data on their impact. Use A/B testing or user analytics to objectively measure whether the changes have addressed the identified issues and improved the overall user experience. Adjust or iterate further based on the collected data.

Communicate Changes to Users: Keep your users informed about the improvements being made to the product. Communicate the changes through release notes, email newsletters, or in-app notifications. This not only informs your users about the improvements but also shows that you value customer feedback and are actively working to address their concerns.

Collect New Feedback: Once the improvements are implemented, continue to gather feedback on the changes to ensure they are meeting the desired objectives. Use this feedback to further refine and iterate on your product, creating a continuous feedback loop that drives ongoing improvement.

Continuous evaluation and improvement are essential for the success and growth of your product in today's competitive market. By actively seeking customer feedback, monitoring business metrics, and continuously iterating on your product, you can ensure that it remains relevant, valuable, and user-centric. Implementing strategies for continuous improvement within your organization and fostering a culture of learning and feedback will allow you to stay ahead of the competition, maximize customer satisfaction, and drive sustained growth for your business. Remember, the journey towards improvement is a continuous one, and by embracing it, you p

Building, Launching, and Succeeding with a SaaS Business

Building and launching a SaaS (Software-as-a-Service) business can be an exciting and rewarding endeavor. However, it requires careful planning, execution, and continuous improvement to ensure long-term success. In this conclusion, we will summarize the key elements discussed in the previous chapters that are essential for building, launching, and succeeding with a SaaS business.

Chapter 1: Understanding the SaaS Model
The first step in building a successful SaaS business is understanding the SaaS model itself. SaaS is a software distribution model where customers access software applications over the internet, rather than installing and maintaining software on their own servers. Key takeaways from this chapter include:

Scalability and Accessibility: SaaS allows for easy scalability and accessibility, making it an attractive choice for businesses of all sizes.

Subscription Pricing: SaaS typically utilizes a subscription pricing model, providing recurring revenue and predictable cash flow for your business.

Customer-Centric Approach: SaaS businesses must prioritize customer satisfaction and provide ongoing value to retain customers.

Chapter 2: Identifying a Market and Target Audience
To succeed in the SaaS industry, it is crucial to identify a market and target audience with a

strong need for your product. Key takeaways from this chapter include:

Market Research: Thoroughly research the market, competitors, and customer needs to identify a gap that your SaaS product can fill.

Niche Targeting: Focus on a specific target audience and niche, rather than trying to appeal to a broad market. This allows for better customization and customer-centricity.

Value Proposition: Clearly define your unique value proposition that sets you apart from competitors and resonates with your target audience.

Chapter 3: Designing and Developing Your SaaS Product
Designing and developing a high-quality SaaS product is crucial for success. Key takeaways from this chapter include:

User-Centric Design: Prioritize user experience and design a product that is intuitive, user-friendly, and solves specific pain points for your target audience.

Agile Development Methodology: Adopt agile development practices to enable flexibility, faster iterations, and adaptability to changing market needs.

Quality Assurance: Implement rigorous quality assurance processes to ensure your product is bug-free, stable, and meets customer expectations.

Chapter 4: Pricing, Monetization, and Revenue Strategy
Determining the right pricing and revenue strategy is essential to generate sustainable revenue and maximize profitability. Key takeaways from this chapter include:

Value-Based Pricing: Determine the value your product provides to customers and set pricing that reflects that value.

Flexible Pricing Tiers: Offer multiple pricing tiers with different features and benefits to cater to a wide range of customer needs and budgets.

Pricing Iteration: Continuously evaluate and adjust your pricing strategy based on market feedback, customer behavior, and changing market conditions.

Chapter 5: Marketing and Acquiring Customers
Effective marketing and customer acquisition strategies are critical for growing your SaaS business. Key takeaways from this chapter include:

Inbound Marketing: Utilize inbound marketing strategies such as content marketing, SEO, social media, and email marketing to attract and engage your target audience.

Lead Generation: Implement lead generation strategies such as gated content, free trials, and demos to capture and convert potential customers.

Customer Referral Programs: Leverage satisfied customers to drive referral marketing by implementing customer referral programs.

Chapter 6: Customer Onboarding and Retention
Customer onboarding and retention are crucial for the long-term success of your SaaS business. Key takeaways from this chapter include:

Smooth Onboarding Experience: Provide a seamless and intuitive onboarding process to help customers get up and running quickly.

Provide Ongoing Value: Continuously provide value to customers through regular updates, new features, and exceptional customer support.

Proactive Customer Success: Implement a proactive customer success strategy to identify and address customer needs and prevent churn.

Chapter 7: Building a Supportive Company Culture
Creating a supportive company culture is essential for motivating and retaining employees, fostering innovation, and driving the success of your SaaS business. Key takeaways from this chapter include:

Clear Mission and Values: Establish a clear mission and set of values that guide your company's actions and decisions.

Empowerment and Collaboration: Encourage employee empowerment and foster a collaborative environment where ideas and feedback are valued.

Continuous Learning and Growth: Support employee development through regular training, learning opportunities, and growth-oriented performance evaluations.

Chapter 8: Continuously Evaluate and Improve Your Product

Continuous evaluation and improvement are crucial to meeting customer needs, staying ahead of competitors, and driving sustained growth. Key takeaways from this chapter include:

Identify Areas for Improvement: Regularly evaluate business metrics and gather customer feedback to identify areas of your product that require enhancement.

Implement Agile Development Practices: Break down your product roadmap into smaller, manageable increments to enable quick iterations and incorporate customer feedback.

Monitor User Analytics: Utilize user analytics tools to gain insights into user behavior and iteratively improve the overall user experience.

By incorporating these key elements into your strategy, you can set yourself up for success in building, launching, and growing your SaaS business. While each chapter focused on specific aspects, it is important to remember that these elements are interconnected and should be implemented holistically for the best results.

The journey of building and succeeding with a SaaS business requires continuous learning, adaptation, and improvement. Stay agile, listen to your customers, and be proactive in addressing their needs. By doing so, you can

build a thriving SaaS business that delivers
ongoing value, delights customers, and achieves
long-term success.

Notes:

www.ingramcontent.com/pod-product-compliance
Lightning Source LLC
Chambersburg PA
CBHW071104260726

48661CB00006B/2458